HOROLOGY

DEREK

HOROLOGY

GROMADZKI

SHEARSMAN BOOKS

First published in the United Kingdom in 2021 by
Shearsman Books Ltd
PO Box 4239
Swindon SN3 9FN

Shearsman Books Ltd Registered Office
30–31 St. James Place, Mangotsfield, Bristol BS16 9JB
(this address not for correspondence)

www.shearsman.com

ISBN 978-1-84861-740-7

Design: Joshua Unikel

Copyright © Derek Gromadzki, 2021, All rights reserved

The right of Derek Gromadzki to be identified as the author of this work has been asserted by him in accordance with Section 77 of the Copyright, Designs and Patents Act 1988.

Acknowledgments:
Thanks to the editors of the following publications, in which much of the work that follows first appeared, provisionally titled and often much differently arranged: *American Literary Review*; *Barn Owl Review*; *Bayou*; *Bellingham Review*; *BOAAT*; *Chattahoochee Review*; *Seneca Review*; *Sonora Review*; *Spittoon*; *Tokyo Poetry Journal*; *Upstairs at Duroc*; *Wave Composition*; and *Witness*.

The first movement of "Ephemeris" was published as a limited-edition pamphlet under the title *Horology* by Paradigm Press in 2016. Selections of the "Epilogue" were first published by *Fugue* under the title "Echolalia" and later reprinted in celebration of National Poetry Month for the Cuyahoga, OH County Library's "30 Days of Poetry Project."

Completion of this book was made possible in part by a generous grant from the National Endowment for the Arts and the Japan-US Friendship Commission. For which: unstinting gratitude.

This is a work of fiction; its debts are history's.

CONTENTS

Prologue   9

Ephemeris   19

The Log from the Solander Box   29

Ephemeris   45

The Log from the Solander Box   55

Ephemeris   71

The Log from the Solander Box   81

Epilogue   99

Vouchsafe, sweet shipwrecks,
weeks of gentle evenings
in the moments while we drown.

PROLOGUE

Imagine an azimuth in an imagined way. Imagine a line
and let it be bent, a silverstring kink in a showman's
rope strung from two petals of a compass rose.

Call the line a cipher. It slants. It slants fugato and fails.
Call its direction a center on loan from peripheries and
say it escapes itself up a penknife altitude to parallax.

Between is and was is a flicker: the smaller of two suns a
sextant feeds to a miniature sea. You say meridians.
Let's make a list of illusions. That's one.

I say meander and say the tropics are vagaries that tilt out of true. The ecliptic, a carafe's hip a half second of arc abseils, and only the equator is real.

Look for longitude in the length of a wave but look for length in nothing. I say I've heard it said that it rides leviathan chines and steers by parallels of broken hulls.

Of latitude let's speak crosswise of ink on ink, edges and pages from portolan charts. Imagine a ship sails over ellipses and an ellipse undoes an edge with little ado.

Say from the ship circumference is faience, *sine qua* frit and *non* save blue. Say what heading you will for the ship, but I say headwinds and permanent red.

Cerise by west by weathercraft. A sounding bell cedes to fathoms and halves. Call 'by the board' and count deep six a half a dial's worth of time. Next, say dials are days.

Then number hours their cantons. Let minutes chamfer the hours that minutes misfit. Secondhand tangents lever the ship in circles. It finds its way by a watch.

There are tables to chart courses by Jupiter's moons. Hatchmarks, plumbago, and hoaxes! The promise of moons is misconception.

Some sailors count miles by cannon shot. Some starve ravens and set them free for land. Others ask their routes of oracles who never know oceans for staring at stars.

Would you follow the cries of the Lorelei…? Castaway pleas and the shriek of sad epistles leaked from chopines come to pieces on far away cliffs.

The colures may crisscross the poles. But X marks the anonym, a hapax for the shanty man, a spot among flotsam and the rocks that caused the wreck.

North or South, East or West, each has its share of epithets. And no matter. Call them what you will. I call them four fairweather airts not fair in any weather.

I've heard of islands where fishermen lie prone in pitch paper canoes, commune with currents by touch, and direction is a prose tattoo down a helmsman's back.

And I've heard of batik shadows on sailcloth that come alive wayanging where the wax gives way to point the wayward home. But say me no lessons of the lost at sea.

Of their improvised prayers, of their lodestone agalma and their legerdemain. How many fata morganas mistaken for Maida? How many hulks trawled hard aground?

Apparitions founder. And travelers, they founder after apparitions all the same. Suppose a vision only masquerades as real, or that it forgets to be untrue.

That visions move as the counterworld without moves, too. And time begins in motion. That the yaw in a squall admits what memory allots the squall to admit.

And no more. Gather your remainders and buoy the lagan. Overboard, both. Wish them liquid halidoms, haint shades of sloe and stygian blacks.

Up backwash, up brine! Fetch a spare breath from a wineskin lung and know that here the needful things you keep will haunt you.

Gitane, the breakers that bewry a windup ship.
Imagine whirlwinds flying witches' kites louver its sails.
Think quiver is the answer they give and stow away.

A rhumb line of thunderheads. Aubergine pennons of
vapor with a cutthroat edge approach the moments just
after after. A black jasper gale. *Exeunt omnes*. To the hatches.

Riffle your thoughts and think whipcord. The rigging
reveilles a skeleton crew. Look, spyglass obols fixed to
their eyes. Sternway, sternway the naufrage… plunge on.

EPHEMERIS

*Tempus item per se non est, sed rebus ab ipsis
consequitur sensus, transactum quid sit in aevo,
tum quae res instet, quid porro deinde sequatur;
nec per se quemquam tempus sentire fatendumst
semotum ab rerum motu placidaque quiete.*

Lucretius

A thumb smudge and a   shudder
    of knuckle play about the hinge
oil arabesques on a windmill
inside a cylinder
                 anchored to all
           the weight of anything
        that never weighed at all.

    Somewhere an aquarelle château
and a countess – ribbons in chignon
               and a lapis pin –
walks patterns sub-
     tending intarsia
         in her winter garden
              wears a little clock
              in a telescope
tube around her neck   and dreams
of wings perhaps and
paradox.

                    She'll say she heard that
                            things with wings
                                like windmills
only seem to fly
she heard   that
arrows   like wings
for all their feathers   are   fixed
                         in   place
or place is a change that annexes
change
stuck coming forward in circles: the
clockwork bluebells in a burning glass
                    on a papered wall
                where she tilts the tube
off kilter and sundown rigs the lens –
a convex lantern
cast onto Toile de Jouy at crepuscule
– as if outward from herself were east

and on the wall   *tick-*
                tick   antinomies
                         of instants   spin
                         at sixes and sevens:
no points   but
a prism's   faultlines
confined   in rotary motion appliqué
                  a tinny metronome
      affianced to afterglow.

One   footfall
luciform on varnish
begins a memory –
buttons she counts backwards
        from mother of pearl
                to the ormering tides
                   outing ormer shells
    salt air and something like indigo
    up to her shins

– a color of sea that was that
cannot be
so the sea surrenders
        to verdigris –
an overcast
like ormolu
worn where the green shows through
last seen in
the space between the space between
        lead leaving a leadlight
and quartet reflections of four o'clock.

Another step is a slipper waylaid
in a series of slippers and al-
ways partway less than one
        and already later
    in a past the present precedes
where time will lay its arrow down
beside itself.

Then would
that   would
        were   is
                    and she would stay
                        when she was
                                once
– if seasons were whin and blackberry
bits of road
detours   to
            sundial driftwood stood
                    in the sand
and hours no taller than a girl is small.

            She said a prayer to shade she
            wrote a wish on foolscap
            and threw it to the wind:
I might
I may –
a violin wasp carried her wish away.

A handiwork hum   it   was
                 a   lullaby
lived in her ear and breathed
vibrato a   breath
a quavering   now
            now   tuning fork ferns
                rehearse an antode's
   opposite song an open window ex-
   hales
   from a parterre
        aperture in false perspective
and so much of the same is the same
she thinks
          as the wrong difference and
                what difference
       divides   seconds   from
       soutache
       or stiches in minutes

               a pocket full of nine   any nine
               from any number   for   rags
               or tags and
                              patches
before numbers fumble over
safety-
pin pinpricks and fibula snags   a few
more than a few stalks of thread that
bellwether fray   pleats   deciphered
                       by   pantomimes
and pirouettes   or bullion fretwork
on a furbelow
         looted
         in the shadow of a chandelier
                  hung from a candle –
black   on black lacquer
a chronograph   set to drag
dragging years   across the floor.

Syncope   stops short of turning back
         a short   stay on the peri-
meter   she'll say of otherwise
and lets relation have its way with
unrelated parts of afternoons
apart from empty
                 spaces and the
              forms and shapes
area makes to shape a life in rooms.

A crooked kind of edgeless-
                      ness
interior to steam has capered and will
between tealeaves and tealeaf dust a
gearworks winds down a duet
for dauphine hands she
rewinds and nickel inflicted on nickel
        overhauls   another   matins
                  again.

THE LOG FROM THE SOLANDER BOX

— *from the notebooks of John Harrison, clockmaker*

Audavi a quodam homine docto, quod solis et lunae ac siderum motus ipsa sint tempora et non adnui.

Augustine

So little for looking. Barely albedo in sixpence pools. Sound's blind sight clearer than wet reflections from the quay. This lanternless kalends. Chiaroscuro more obscure for fog. Intermittent the slap and damp shatter of water on barnacled wood. Fainter but uninterrupted a thousand dull thuds all at once. Our oilskins wick away a light rain. Leather footsteps shuffle three-four on the dock below, the ship's deck above. A gangway of steep planks shrilly giving between them. Upward the ballast and heavier loads. Pulleys milling salt around rusted axels. Coir tight as pig iron stretched between basso and a cricket's chirp. The crates it girdles noiseless. As if their heft offset their measure in rumor and bruit. Trundle alow. Strained inhalations. Two wharf men turn a treadwheel crane. Like dropsy one to the other the descant they wheeze.

Enceinte the ship. Rough the metal peal of mooring cleats relieved of their lines. Chirruped returns from hawser rings. Away and dim we sluice. Aft to fore some seventy feet neither carrack nor cog tracing oxbow tenebrae on demimonde time. Past stippled chimneypots reared against manufactory fog. Past fish scales pinchbeck aglimmer where neap mud grouts the cobblestone walks rucked into the river's banks. Harbor to sound to sea.

Oceanward. And oceangoing still a sinecure for frauds and figurists who apportion the world in circles they square.

During the reign of Antoninus Pius, the atlas Ptolemy compiled contained twenty- seven maps overlaid with coordinate grids he'd cribbed from Persian gazetteers. Half hearsay, half complete, his geography extended east from Rome to Cattigara and westward back to Hy-Brasil. Thereafter, dragons.

In a hemisphere of best guesses, Ptolemy's maps gave voyagers unreliable latitudes and vexed them with longitudes based on surmises.

Cartographers played a game of make-believe with the no-places of no-man's-land and believed they were real enough.

Here is the whole world in all its length and width, reads the legend on the *Erdapfel* that Martin Behaim built in 1491. To which he added Tracoda, a land of men who ate snakes and spoke only in hisses. And the mysterious lake isle of Silha, formed from a valley where Adam and Eve spent one hundred years weeping.

Entering an age of globes, mariners sailed an orthogonal world.

They made posthaste for the parallel where their destination lay, hewing that line for all they had, and set a watchman to surveil the sky. Up at *lauds*, agog amidships. A quondam bowsprit bent double over the gunwale. Begging Heaven for the heavens' ways with a fore-staff aimed at *ignes fatui*. Distant shimmers past the farthest outposts of the air. Pale fanals through a glasseye view. Empires have steered by such beacons as these.

Acute cutwater and the dogwatch hours. Subfusc cumulus. Holier hues become mundane. Overhead, calico sheets lax and smacking like clobbered drumheads daven arrhythmic in the yardarms of the mainmast. Whitecaps rake lather along the carvel planks. They heave and subside and crest again. Argent babble. Marled gunmetal and chop.

Tracking latitude at sea consists in little, excepting the record of apices and waiting around for noon. Location by longitude has been a problem. It persists to date.

In the beginning was Eratosthenes. At the foot of an obelisk. Sheltered in the seven meagre degrees of shade that midday affords in Alexandria and contemplating the length of the same shadow he saw, were it cast in Syene. He solved the world's circumference.

Five-thousand stadia, he figured.

Hardly more.

Latitude's radius rules the value of longitude's degrees. *Caeteris paribus* and safe from the poles, where coordinate pairs close in on themselves, somewhere about the planet's middle middle, say. There's an hour either side of every fifteen degrees. Minutes measure the miles. And seconds count feet ten to the dozen.

But anon the wick-trimmer to tend to the lamps.

His face a yellow mask in the whale oil glow going before him. A yellow jaundiced in lieu of gold.

He lifted the globe from off my lamp and pared the wick while he kept it alight.

Crammed in my cabin, spare parts from dismantled clocks. Fusée chains, levers laid out in trays. Minute screws, my tools, my springs, and brass axels like quills. Calculations for torque that cover the trusses.

Transfixed to see such fragile things undone. He said he'd sailed indefinite tours and poured his oils and kindled lamps. His look a saccade. From my bench then back to me then back. He ventured conjectures he'd heard of a pilot watch. Or watches. From where he wasn't able to say. One estaminet bay begins, ends, and begins to resemble the next.

A clock, I told him. *Yes*.

To transfigure time for place. A clock to right meridians and obsolesce the distance to the moon.

I told him. A frigate bound for Hastings. Bleak forecast, once upon a thunderclap.

Enter gusts, insurmountable swells. Trust the pilot, the pilot implores the captain. He cleaves a sextant's course transcribed in lunars. By any other name, crude angles that he swindled from the moon.

Frantic, scrap paper reckoning. Impromptu and pitchpoling toward the Channel Islands. Ushant, it should have been, to slack anchors for sanctuary.

From here, I told him, *you'll know the tale.*

The sextant's eye concenters the storm's. Neither *navia* nor *caput*, the pilot can't make heads or tails of his bearings. When the boatswain swears he sees sour figs growing against the ashen granite of Cornish Scilly where he learned to steer a skiff, the pilot has the captain have him hanged. A mutineer. Commits his body, knocking from the crosstrees, to gusts.

Headlong, vessel and crew, into the looming crags. The prow splayed open. As undone as the rotted, bitter ends of a rope. Drowned seamen like knots and snags along the gnarled kern inside it. And the captain alone survives. He kicks, flails. He fights and ebbs forward on a flowing tide. From his knees on the beach he gasps for help. Mayhap he prays. Rag-pickers cut him neck to navel for his emerald ring.

Afterdeck. A ledger line horizon. Terns cry toward the firmament. Lesser sharps amid felled figure threes receding.

A clockbox carriage house upon a hill.

Strange a box should serve safekeeping best. Coffers for writs. Chests for coins. Mappemondes in aumbries. All and sundry shapes for clocks.

And the first clockbox that I recall was a carriage house upon a hill. Its door sealed shut, carved into a dial. The dial inlaid with hour sticks of alloyed scrap. A pair of sickle blades burnished and straightened for hands. I recall it ran backwards the whole day long, and roughly. Rancid soap it must have been, instead of oil inside the works. It never rang but to break. Chainlinks snapped. Counterweights fallen akimbo.

I remember. Sick in bed a boy with pocks, I carved a three in a burl from a pockwood tree. A three would be a bird I thought. But another beside it made it eight and eight gave way to fever. Every number was one. Was a tangent. A sum: two rings touching. Two rings, I thought, that might be ragged wheels. Fever. Fetid sheets, and I whittled.

Where the wood slivers fell, fever's scent acceded. Incense nearly, not quite clematis. Oil in sap's stead. Weak vanilla cut with fresh cut turf. Sweet and slick as either. Frictionless, larded from within, the rings rolled in my hands. Lacinate, side by side where they'd had more metal, cog to tooth and misbegot, the rings were gears. Gears to turn the gears to turn the hands of a constant clock. Gears to chew the moon to scattershot. Or I invented it all. A child dismantles his father's watch.

Straightaway and clang, wild bell! A church bell I remember. Doubtful westwork. Entering right, the tower stout below the campanile and hourly played chute to its clangor. Left, the other bell, the rightside's twin, lay in a fallen ziggurat of mortar, of brick. Of adamant, for all I knew. The old squire lay under the rubble. It's said he's like to have vanished under a weight so many magnitudes beyond the little he displaced. Turvy the bronze bell top had lumbered down and lay his cenotaph across the ground.

That I should be a tinker for a broken tower, be a ringer for a fallen bell. When buildings unbuilt already rose. Or with Roman walls mid-topple still crenellating hills that front Hadrian's retreat. Here lining a drainage trench. Stacked there, repurposed for a shithouse bothy. Noble ignoble stuff, the detritus.

Fissured bricks. The fractured whitebeam. Easily a season's cords of mothy poplar. Unannealed nails clotted with mal-cured resin reeking gangrene through the joists. Solemn nods. Little spoken. Solemn for heaps, for cave-ins, collapses. Solemn for the finders of piecemeal things. And a testate commission for a tower clock. The lignum vitae that would be its bones. Felled, floated, and hauled from Müritz.

In passing weeks we knapped the cluttered stones and piled the viable blocks. Stacked them by cut. Collected the dross and combustibles best we could. Split stair planks. Halved ladder rungs. Then, pockets full of nails, we lit the fires.

Ashes to echoes and smoke lent echoes extra inches to the arcs of their necks. Scorched, sooty footlights crying for curtains up. Absent intermission, the marionette errands.

A tower case as good as any frame to reinforce the works. The work to support the works. Carpenters, masons. Joiners and stonecutters leering red-eyed through their respective dusts. A pendulum like a tree and chimes for hangmen's bones to swing from the branches. Cogs as large as wagon wheels. A rude choreography, a rehearsal, for dancing figurines to speak, if speak they could, to onlookers looking on, *look up no higher than here and recollect to wake to labor to revel to rest.* And I, plumbed from a harness, fontoche at work inside the walls. Assessments, measurements, and estimations. Remeasurements. Skinflint scaffolds for just fingers and toes. Misplaced parts. Unfailingly the light a marble *dämmerung*. Like restoring a raided tomb.

But how many times have you heard this?

I still remember everything that followed. Undone by hand from living wood. Then done to live again.

I sanded bearings one by one. Drilled bushings, planed rollers with a razor blade. From the winding arbors behind the dial, like a worm I sapped wafers of fluted wheels for rhizomes of screws. And at the center, vivisection to make it live. A fiddlestick grasshopper poised and dancing on the head of a pin. Plucked, and plucks now, frantic at the pallets of its own heart with the plectra on its legs. For no other occasion. For the occasion it keeps.

Once, hereafter was dovetails and cherry slats. To think that it's come to this.

Some thirteen hundred years ago Norsemen mined a kind of quartz and called it sunstone. An invalided *völva*, a seer priestess, had swallowed her tongue to prophecy that peering through the crystal from the prow of a longship would show the crew safe passage to wherever they wished.

We put to sea and with only Mercury to guide us we arrived at your kingdom, said Hergist the Saxon.

That a watch could run lockstep with the sun.

Ides already. Ideal for reckoning pitfalls. The crashes and comings-apart. The abandonments that buttress history's ends.

Here'll be one I haven't told. During the Spanish Succession, the HMS Prydwen was a sixty-gun ship of the line. South-southwest while rounding Cape Horn she ran into waterspouts. Tall swells. Fleet bubbles like breath in the troughs. Buffeted hard. Invisibility. Impact. Having tacked this way instead of. And hard aground on the Chilean coast.

The crew descended the hull's fissured ribs. Reached safety, conferred, and scattered. The Spanish salvaged enough of what remained to wright a makeshift sloop. To outfit it with the Prydwen's own plundered guns. Boat and cannons both sent back to war against their makers.

Said Heraclitus, *out of everything, a unified whole and out of a unified whole, everything.*

Why should symmetry elicit the awe that it does?

Let's lay the blame with Pythagoras and his initiates. With their mysteries. As among us, *a fortiori*, so too in lines of music made among the spheres. Or so the mysteries go. His eavesdroppers apprenticed to smithies, auditing hammerfalls on anvils for arcaner equations to crack enciphered skies. Their solfège a spherical book writ large, cosmos and crystal quires, tethered with an outré clef, *primum mobile*, between an *F* and a *G*.

I shouldn't get carried away.

But take the number four. For instance. Sometime long ago, when geometry and mantic were one and the same, a student approached his rabbi. *Hakham*, he said. *What does it mean?*

The first coupling coupled, the rabbi replied. *Four matriarchs. Four kingdoms of the eschaton. Revelation's four horsemen, four angels, four beasts, and four winds.*

Four elements.

Four cardinal directions, too. And who'd believe in imbalance among them? Though it's there.

Latitude courses north or south. Longitude spreads east, west, and lacks a natural point of reference. Like the equator. Though Hipparchus proposed one at Rhodes.

From Plato, we inherit a quiescent earth nested in a needle's eye. Necessity's spindle, and flux all around it spun by three Fates.

We must imagine the stellar sphere at rest, wrote Jean Buridan, *then night and day will ensue from the movement of the earth.* Unless I'm mistaken, Louis X had him clapped in irons, stuffed in a sack, and cast into the Seine.

With no landmarks, determining longitude by celestial means, as needs must at sea, depends upon the turning of the earth.

A turning that's time as we know it.

It's not that time hove out from zero like a flood among us and took us away. It's that a few monsoon chasers stayed, surveyed the flood, and from the flood's withdrawal inferred our time. Plowmen and pushcart merchants. The first to fathom and keep it. Accidental vintners. Potters. Net fishers among the marshes. Decocted labor from seasons of living. To assess, to jar and barrel gestures performed *seriatim*, out of sorts with their own sequelae.

From tortue redoubts to perfumers' souks. They wrote compass carrefours across a flatter earth. Then came and made a commerce of the sea. Itinerant profiteers waged omphalos wars for centers on the surface of a sphere.

Phillip II of Spain, sobriquet the Prudent, established a prize in 1598 worth one hundred thousand crowns payable to anyone who could overcome the longitude conundrum. Not to be outdone, a principal directive of the *Académie royale des sciences* that Louis XIV founded in 1666 was to outbid other nations for theorists who showed the greatest aptitude in improving cartography and advancing the study of navigation.

Open invitations for crackpots and bedlam. I'd say just think of the impractical applications proposed for everyday things, but they beggar reckoning. From alum to cannonballs, to scullery salts and vitriol.

Avaricious captains on the take to enterprise. Dragging their crews toward fey infinities. Impoverished conscripts, volunteers without a better choice. All fools, however they go, and slaughtered among their misgivings.

EPHEMERIS

Dum tamen hanc sperat, dum praecorrumpere donis me cupit, elige, ait virgo Cumaea, quid optes: optatis potiere tuis. Ego pulveris hausti ostendens cummulum, quot haberet corpora pulvis, tot mihi natales contingere vana rogavi; excidit, ut peterem iuvenes quoque protinus annos.

Ovid

There are rhythms
and there are rhythms
some are cock's crow tomorrows
            like tomorrow
          sure to…
some
      are charades and they disappear
            wherever ever after is.

            Clair de lune
             syllables of
caravels lap a chlorodyne shore
half
a bottle half
      liqueur like baize and
portmanteau chant partial to none –
an ocean in an ampoule once she
thinks upon a time became the time
    but once upon will never do.

    Or   if   there is a once upon
   it's nothing   that it used to be –
how a model ship is a whirligig
that wasn't –
                a ship under way
                to   nowhere
                      where
    it sails
back to itself
between   it-
self and   its   image   bending
                    in a demijohn
                toward a bottleneck
tied off and
liable to choke on the twine.

She stirs the figure she thinks
    an echo makes with one finger
                  in the air

                and in the air
                the upper air
the ether where she dreams she sees
another   ship
afloat around the planets she counts
                one   two... afloat
on horn shavings
from the moon.

            Upward in abysm
                   mal-de-mer
        among the magnified:
milk lights like brief insects precess
the equinox
           and
    scribble
    new abscissa
    to myths that
    circumscribe the stars myths

                    that begin
            with myths of beginnings
              and from the ship   she
thinks she
hears
she   hears
a   chanticleer of fo'c'sle songs
singing an unseen cage of
                            wire en-
compassed the earth and bygone
gods played loss upon it like a crwth.

              She swivels
crescent   surveys across
the zodiac
                  and her sightline
            caroms off constellations
littered with upended argosies   their
scuttled   keels like   crosses.

Sotto voce   and she recites a lay
of two fish –   one
aswim   with another
      amid disjecta from a spalted
hulk   – two fish that took
two ends
of severed rigging in
their mouths and towed away
two lovers clinging to a ruined boom.

          Years   ago she lost track
         how many
                  agos ago it was
                 she contracted
     half the village
to have the village build
a copper   hemisphere
     on the highest   echaugette
            of her   château.

                    The dome
        a metal exponent leftover from pi
        given the third degree
        a primer for lichen
                            and hewn
        clean through with a sickle fenêtre
        opening on a looking glass
                as long as a man –
                            the whole
                    vault slowly aspin
                on shaky casters and nightly
            she waits beneath it
        with a solander box and phials
        divers casebottles of onetime
        tonics and hydromel
                incongruent pitkins and   flasks
                curating
                            misbegotten codicils.

She married a man in love with time
or she married a man in love with her
in love
   with time he sailed away
and sometimes bottles came back.

From the village around the château
       rumors
  after his absence
 besieged her and when
she listened she could hear
       acoustic
       analemmae
     of her own name
   helix
    through alleys
in louche banlieues and curl
where villagers discarded odds
and ends for indigents

     and ambled
  wagging their chins at one
another and used to wonder if
they'd ever lure the countess
from her hermitage
and how.

    She'd kept a routine of strict
tristesses until a whelked and
pitted mallet jug
      dibbled in the surf
and jangled clumsy on pebbles up-
shore in a storm – inside in a script
that skipped on a note
addressed to her a note she read it said
    sixty seconds' worth of ticks
  and twenty-six sounds are not enough
  but said no more except
      for water rings.

THE LOG FROM THE SOLANDER BOX

— *from the notebooks of John Harrison, clockmaker*

Alius quidam veterum poetarum, cuius nomen mihi nunc memoriae non est, Veritatem Temporis filiam esse dixit.

Gellius

Intemperate today. A barleywine aubade. Meerschaum and broderie anglaise immingle. Salamander wool incoming with the westerlies. Audible scumble in the offing. Tarred paulins battened over the hatchway grates.

Below-decks I sit. I listen. Far up, from the crow's nest, an Aeolian harp coughs tuneless. Quinsy through the royals and rigging.

Epigone replicas for the Tower of Winds.

On into dun. A watcher at the taffrail besotted by spume. Have I mentioned him yet? I stay my hand to write his name.

O, my dear prelate.

And how should I call him, my keeper, the cuss? A poor possessor letting go. His god wound up the universe and walked away.

Above Kêr Ys there was the aerodrome. An outlook pied with airships. Hierophant captains aboard their balloons inventing apogees. The crude quinquennia they sacrificed to sunbeams. *Avale*, they pled. *Avale, avale a virelay! Sing a new prayer to timists.*

Time heretofore in the hands of clerisies.

When Francis Xavier's mission reached Japan, he bribed the *daimyo* with matchlock rifles. And clocks.

It's said Paracelsus fused saffron and pearls, crabs' eyes and butterfly scales into a powder close in composition to the spirit of the world. The formula passed to Carmelite monks who discovered that, applied to any substances of shared atoms, it transmitted stimuli equally among them. Heedless how far apart.

Imagine burning across oceans.

Did I ever tell you? When Parliament passed the Longitude Act, offering rewards upwards of twenty-thousand pounds to any and all, they entertained a proposal from an ostiary who said he possessed a 'powder of sympathy.' The very same.

He planned to suspend it in a salve of boar's fat. His other requests were few. A bistoury, a dog and its keeper. He'd open an incision in the dog. Wipe the salve on the wound. Then send cur and keeper out to sea. Every day at noon he'd slather the blade with the salve and subject it to fire. *Instanter*, back on the ship, the dog would cry out. Plus or minus local time, and lo! Let the ship's location be known.

Of course. And we the ignorant go on to ignorance. Elsewhere as we can.

Crumhorns peal. Up, unholy *incipit*.

Tars and press-ganged marinels. Clined and tripoded, two knees to an elbow, they crank chamois hands on rocksalt and sand to polish the deck laths he'll pace.

Our priest, as his predecessors. Clerics, astronomers royal, keepers of clocks and measures. Makers of none.

Deus providebit.

He insists that longitude confounds solution. Knowing it, he says, assays the mind of God.

Said Nicholas of Cusa, *God constitutes the center of the universe. Indeed,* wrote al-Iji once from the observatory at Samarqand, *events above overlap events below in a nexus of gossamer orbs finer than daydreams or spiders' silk.*

Throw away your parti pris, he's implored me, *and think of the moon. Is it so unlike the hand of a clock? The sky its dial, with stars for indices?*

Every hour on the hour the moon traverses its width. One single incident the same *passim*. But his answer's an enigma in an almanac still being written. Drawn across cities and ports of call, the moon's paths across the ecliptic. Whoever sees them, though, sees them askew.

So look up, right where you are. Measure the moon by a reference star. Correct for parallax. Refer to imperfect tables yet in the making. Take the difference in hours between you and the nearest known point on land. Multiply by fifteen degrees and repeat sevenfold for accuracy's sake. You'll have found your longitude.

Meanwhile beam seas assault the sheerstrake, your ship rolls, and forward you heave.

Wanted: one silver book a year in length, each page a golden day.

Arthritic, he crowded his paunch upwise a companion ladder. Vim and a shove, save vigor, through a crippled hatch propped on a mop handle. Above it, harrumphing, a vision in cassock, bilge fringe, and Canterbury cap when I caught the uppermost rung.

Saltimbanque incumbents. A plate-spinning circus of sextants fitted to quadripods. Spotters wearing amber spectacles and in file behind them scriveners with ledgers open on their laps. Cuttlefish gall overspilled their inkwells. Up step and down step through it. Ballet paces preserved in gouache.

We sue one another for a separate truth, the priest and I. And the spolia? Quiet revolution, a moment's repute. I've turned his Father Time into a pinwheel toy. I've trapped him in a box.

I told him the Shah of Isfahan had a mechanical feather in the form of a bird.

I asked whether he'd read the Portuguese reports from the *Nanban* trade on the *yukaku* of Nagasaki. The pleasure districts where ornately japanned *tansu*, trunks with puzzlebox compartments, stand in a corner of every ill-reputed house's every room. Of no impetus their own, the trunks open. Enameled hands emerge and tap bejeweled bells affixed beneath their lids. Intimately announcing the conclusion of an evening's, an afternoon's. However long the leisure of a few copper coins.

You'll know, I inquired, *the legends of Albertus Magnus and the disembodied skulls, the skulls the legends say that he made talk?*

And you'll recall the abdicated, apostate queen, Christina of Sweden? Virago, they said, a jezebel. She secretly received Athanasius Kircher in Stockholm on the eve of her flight to Rome. Among the persuasions he made for her was this. Flayed and tanned gobbets of flesh from condemned men's hides stitched taut across the grains of a rosewood pome he'd scooped out for eyes, hollowed for a mouth with a hinge and a jaw that moved. Inside, an impossible lattice. Diminutive windlasses, sprockets, and strings. Concealed in the cheeks, a choir of valves for drawing breath and pipettes tuned to exhale it like speech. A rawhide tongue wrapped around a wire to control the stops.

Had he heard, I wondered, the latest news from Holland. Of Kleist in Leyden ginning lighting in a jar?

Hark, I told him. *A quiet, highbeat tremolo. It's the clockmakers marching with gifts.*

Rasping, the spray outside. Exhale, inhale, and *chante cigale*.

I can't help but hear coveys of citrine finches. Exaltations of larks.

They sang while you chivied out the best medlars from the medlar tree and tossed them to me for bletting.

And when the medlar died I saved a block from the trunk I sawed away. I built a music box. Finger joints and a lid that cambered with a fingerprint whorl. You told me I'd bewitched the tree and made of it my hands.

Hammer and tongs, I set studs into a disc of steel. A crank's turn, and it scattered a clutch of lamellae like wanton rushes. Five times the songbirds from as many Mays.

Did you know, under the agoras of Delos, the island where it's supposed Apollo was born, few of the sundials sold had any markings on them at all? Gnomons and styles indifferent to hours. Revolute shadows intended to simulate control of the sun. Nothing more.

We're soon for somewhere in the New World.

Inclinable to calm. I've been squinting over the broadside. Reflections in the metalwork eddies chase a symphony of lustrous fish.

How far down to Fiddler's Green?

Edmond Halley almost died in a diving bell below the Thames. *Quid iacet infernis.*

When we get there, we're to wait and witness Venus and the sun in conjunction. So the priest will have another key for his codebook. All the better to pinpoint the elusive maid in the moon.

Clear Selene, Hesiod called her.

With that, Helios is brought to heel again. Though the two are only up together half of every month.

But lay that by.

A century and then some since Gemma Frisius dreamed up a solution for longitude dependent on clocks.

The idea spread and when it reached the Collège Royal, Jean-Baptiste Morin, insistent on an astronomical answer, laughed. *The devil may make a longitude clock, but as for men I have my doubts. Surely*, he said, *his is a dream dreamed deep in his cups.*

Haroosh, haroosh, the devil's due.

In the interim, his English competitors pushed soberer schemes. Convinced the Atlantic seafloor nowhere surpassed three hundred fathoms, William Whiston suggested a squadron of sloops moored thirty leagues apart. From Pembroke to the American colonies. Equip the ships with dreadful guns, he recommended. To fire a starburst shell six thousand feet high at the stroke of midnight. Concluding that seafarers for a hundred miles could verify their whereabouts with respect to the flash.

Once or twice I've caught myself. Gawking at my old half hunter with drugged intent. Lengthwise my fingers down the chain. Like I'm telling beads. The lamplight fractures, guilloché, on the bezel around the glass and gives the lie to the pitiable time it keeps, to its every other omitted beat.

It's true. The pendulum clocks that Frisius dreamed of using just wouldn't have worked. Picture time transpiring from a lyre bob. Picture it thrashing in a casket launched on the ocean.

Like the ostiary and Paracelsus's powder. Whose proposition, *pace* logic, relied on reason enough. An accessory to two times. Now and then. Twin whens we use to tell ourselves a where.

Bazaar gates close in Istanbul behind an afternoon's last hagglers toting away carpets and mottled copper finjans. Mourners, greaved in the Ganges's silt, replenish their pitchers, offer diyas to the honored dead. Even then, Siberian whalers are up before sunrise anointing harpoons with rhodiola for luck.

Coterminous. Never the same time.

I can monitor the changeable light where I am. But so far from home, how can I recover what happens at home? Wherever home happens to be.

I sit annotating what can only be yesterdays for you. And while I write, but for a keepsake, I couldn't know whether you've risen from dinner and paused to flatten your palm in the lime pollen on the mantelpiece, or you're already asleep, the sashes open to moths.

Close, I told him. *Keep staring.* Bullion, sultana by turns, the glint that overtook his eyes.

Brass and bronze. Coloratura architecture buzzing seven-eighths an octave above a hush. Cams, flanges, and vanes. Pieces of pieces that barely touch. Except by name, prefix to prefix.

I go padding throughout the ship to keep myself busy. Daily I stop and wind the clock. This morning the priest resolved to come with me. A quarter of our sojourn spent, curiosity won out.

So he saw it. In its guarded cabin, pinned in gimbals, a victim to counting. About the size of a cellaret, secured to a console table held fast to the flooring by bolts through its feet.

He saw the clock's balance fobs sway like antennae. One on either side of a wheel spoked with a pulsing spring that checks the mainspring's release. Interchangeable prate between them.

I told him, *look again and closer.* In the spring, a speed so much itself it mocks the eye with immobility. *Blink a second and think*, I said. *Five beats per blink. Five, the finikin strums.*

In a minute three hundred before a daydream's begun.

Faintly panic grass and taffeta. Rime along the tidemill causeway where we walked. After workbench pursuits, after gimcracks. After daylong, ramshackle failures.

Peripheral din. Millstones, grist. The rush of the weir. Crack willows and river birches bent, recoiling. Leaves led one another unkempt dances to the dying grass.

We wandered upstream and when the tides were right, the sunset only a cresset, we could just see down the penstock. The pond fluming into the tailrace. Clinquant, a waterwheel flapped on its side.

Soughs achill, festooned with simpler rhythms. Paddle strike on paddle strike, chug and tattle.

In a clap it happened and lasted forever. Not a pendulum but a wheel in equipoise with water.

I jammed my hands into my pockets. From my waistcoat I felt my rundown watch jump, waver. Then felt its exta tick erratically away.

A laburnum almacantara leading us on, monotonously on.

Last night the rafters squeaked and jibbered. Dangled in my hammock, I dreamed I was a trill in a repeater chime.

Now the half-hunter's ground to halt. Woeful nota.

I wheedled the nail of my little finger under the caseback lip, just so, and it opened with a demi-flutter. A locket for lockaway seasons. An ouroboros exergue around the cuvette inside that reads *with love: a graven faith in simple things that simple things may last.*

EPHEMERIS

Sapias, vina liques et spatio brevi spem longam reseces.

Horace

Reopen   on a sorry astrophelle
        star clusters like tealeaf
fables she knows lit brightly above her
– carry me murmurs
murmurs
        from across the sea inside
        this upturned cup she thinks
            and retroussé
      par the cutaway
      in the dome
the telescope siphons the night
through a series of mirrors
      in search of
        zero
        where the
log leaves off
unwritten an O *ex*
      nihilo to rebegin.

Orage for chance inversions
to invert chance she pled
orage she pleas to vortices
   and every now
     there comes a flagon
      then a calabash
an amber clavelin with
blood notes on linen
    inside or then again
others incised on bark from curious
trees and wood ash alphabets lost
    among herringbones
  in swatches of twill –
  and she's read
palimpsest forecasts
of favorable retours on slapdash
catamarans from Carib isles
    beneath each one.

            Meaning departs
        from meant to be as time
       reduces to witnessing.

    As soon as she quilts the notes
she collects to make them cohere she
takes them apart
then reshuffles the
                    cuts into prequel
                rhapsodies to conjure
            comelier fortunes from
        a foregoer's spell
and so
I'll… with
halloos and   *water's edge*   then
a scrap of its   own   *answer…*
can be   *I'll [wait] with [the rest,*
            shout] halloos [from the]
water's edge [until we're] answer['d].

                A distance
           out past distance
grew inward
while she accumulated
permutations of ever-was to   keep
its distant ends together and she lived
beleaguered in
              confected air
                    where bottles piled
                            in irrepair –
seeded tinctures feinting
tints that purpled green
          and potstone
                drams of tourmaline –
                every message she coaxed
                          out of the next
was a fragment a figment a trace from
which more traces cascade.

Bewitched by half-sense
inscriptions   come
the fade to day —

                some she bound
                in buckram octavo
some she papered on the walls but
how-
      ever she arranged
        she rearranged them   then
            on and on they kept
coming and overcame her.

              Desiccate   crimped
         they flit away disfigured
butterflies on chill chorales
of sunken oboes from the   bottles'
              mouths   through
        the opening in the dome.

    She wondered where to meet again
                  could be besides
        mementos that such
and such a then was real —
if not in auroras
          not in ripples of quicksilver
           with piebald fiscs if it isn't
a terrace on the darkside of some
satellite
it must
be she thought imminent be-
                tween two
    heirloom ricochets
prior and not yet from one
               second to the next
sliptoeing out of touch   the least
touch that hovers on
withdrawal and

                    in a thrice retreats
          from prodigies toward a trance –
homecomings in spring and
grape   hyacinth
gone as it comes
          acanthus   columns
          and time   told by the leaves
                              of lemon trees
concerts de chambre and
autumn's   browns   a   malmsey
sloshing   bittersweet   beneath
          a   wagon's   wheels –
anywhere but earshot
to colder sounds than winter
                    a white *fromage*
     blancmange not white
   the snow
     while late gets later and long ago.

          Papaverine   sleep
       she owes to yesterday
       and *tenèbres*
extempore
accrue from the *bibelots*
the   bottles the notes repieced
               the fond *objets*
    that unmake her wishes
    make her nowadays
a cadent place
and the past
      a leap
      lentor ashake
           either or neither
high and sideways in a lateral sky
end over end
like an hourglass and only
as long as its next beginning.

THE LOG FROM THE SOLANDER BOX

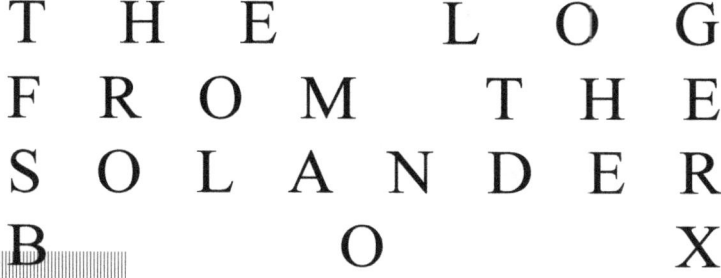

— *from the notebooks of John Harrison, clockmaker*

...*ut laeto tibi tempore tempora uernent, aetatis florem floribus ut decores.*

Apuleius

Lime rinds and cedar. Sweat curing in gabardine. Spilled grog. Salt cod. Varnish. The smells of swim bladders and innards from sundry fish decocted in salves for reproofing sailcloth infuse the sunlight, when it comes. Of honey and perfumed Sirens, nil.

How a scent, too, can tell the time.

Where can it be I read of the architects who planned the Kutubiyya Mosque in Marrakesh? Read they demanded Tonkin musk and agar wood folded into their bricklayers' mortar. This, so the muezzin's calls to Salah would come carried on distinctive odors. Always of fig trees. Then the aromatic beds and perpends scalding between bricks. Subtler in the morning. Most intense in the heat of the day. Vestigial in the eventide.

I remember the mineral tinge. When it rained all the end of August and the paving stones, still hot with summer, shallowly tried to return the rain where it came from.

The antique stalls at Saint-Ouen. We met beneath the eaves. Or under scalloped awnings. A consistent trickle. *One hundred thousand water clocks*, I said.

Hippocras, the color we called the aftermath.

The Nuremburg egg you wore on spiga links. Its cloisonné shell that shone gamboge. A botch of cochineal and aureate jam, dripping *en trein* to nowhere.

Finger-width spindles or trails of santal ash, laced with labdanum. With opopanax. Fuel for the *hidokei*. The fire clocks of Japan.

A typology for two.

Either in the *okiya*, geisha houses, compressed in sticks a half an hour in length and set alight. Where it's said the girls are heard exclaiming *Look! I earned six, seven, eight sticks today.*

Or at temples like the Nigatsudo in Nara. At the water-drawing ceremony, *mizutori*. With the onset of spring, snowmelt from the mountains refills a sacred well. Haggard pilgrims slouch in from miles without. One and all they come carrying tubes to stopper miracles. And six lines of incense slowly burning mete out the day's festivities in equal parts. Torches as long as trees mounted on the balconies shower goodluck cinders on visitors beneath them. Fulgor. Horns blow. Sonnettes ring.

As time applies to the profane so it obtains in the sacred.

Then it was humid and the aqueous balm. The canine fragrance of drenched canvas. Fug from the magpie tramps and junk peddlers in their tents. Their mismatched sets of silver. Whiffs of tarnish hung over their tables.

Chipped porcelain picked up. Put down loudly.

Here.

You cupped the egg to my ear. Told me the clock inside it kept a restive kind of time. *There's some careworn sonnerie in there,* you said, *that's out of place.*

I bought a watch that barely ticked to match. A handheld shambles I wouldn't be bothered to repair. Like the egg, it clanked and jangled.

You told me, *sometimes I lift the lid and turn the hands backwards.*

I thought you walked with bells at your feet and music followed.

The orlop, then berths of sleepers breathing uneasy. Over their heads, a miasma on deck. And damson ignition havers in the mist. So comes the corposant. An optical nocturne scored for sizzling tendrils. Glissando among the windlasses, gaffs, and the foremast men.

A churr shuttles from the lashings, shackles, and pins. The turnbuckles rattle like thunderstruck amphorae. Diminuendo. All their fluid content effervesced.

Petrichor. Pennyweight trickles, not a penny more, incant with a click. Raindrops fountain from the crosstrees, collect in divots where the boards have bowed. Thrip after oxytone thrip. Flimsy refrain.

Deep in the recesses of Solomon's mines, where dusk and dawn were neither and one, stood a cistern carved from living stone. The miners kept their schedules by floating alabaster bowls they'd keyholed to leak and sink by size inside of it.

Clepsydrae, Ktesibios called them. The water thieves. Underground pipettes fed a spigot in his library where he lived beside Lake Mariout. The spigot, a flight of chalices fitted with outflow valves, tiered greatest to least. And to every chalice its paten. Pinned to a scuttling cork, a thimble cloche that tittered when it touched bottom.

Tink. Tink-tink, through the corridors. Iron chinks transmuting, mad as brass. The priest with a book he's chained by its back to his waist.

Staccato. He strides like someone who's never been closer to what remains far, far away. And reads untutored from the pages he cradles chest-high. In rude accents, too. He teedles esoterica that sound like Spain and something else. Stops outside my cabin.

Follow me up to the deck.

At the stern, he jabbed his chin down toward the book. *Twenty-five shlokas*, he told me. Translated *verbatim* by twenty-five outlaw Brahmins. A heretic's treatise on triangulation. Woodcut reproductions of armillary spheres. Retrieved in Toledo. Salvaged from the papists' immolations. Rebound. From Aryabhata's only extant work.

He told me, *in my quest for longitude, I've eschewed sleep to live by night and mortgaged who knows how much of my later life I can't repay.*

Faith will make cowards of us all, he said.

He told me that we live in twisted syllogisms. That there's no escaping them. Tangled skeins we crookedly cleave to. Toward a secret middle we can't conceive.

First, he said, *resigning unbelief for faith entails a total loss. We barter our better selves for something greater. Man is the refuge of defeated men.*

Then through matter, the immaterial. Ours is a living spent clutching the first to presume the latter.

Abrupt, the flutter from a soutane sleeve. His forearm, unhinged at the pivot, flicked for a halyard suspended from the mizzenmast and in his hand it came ablaze. Purpurin volutes iridesced and slid in the dark. There, where he'd snatched the lead, he held the burning of the saints.

A momentary rictus. And then he let it go. Flash and counterflash reared up in abandon.

Not different from St. Elmo's fire. Not body, not void. Tenable though I cannot take it.

In *précis* the rest was this. That we're finite. We do as haste does and consume, leering at how what lasts exceeds us. That time is ours because of all that isn't. That some of what isn't is infinite form.

There occurred a caesura.

The planets' orbits' first impetus for one, he went on. *Riddles meant for others. Not meant for us. Your clock consigns them to snicks and clacks in a pillbox filled with ratchets that run on rules of thumb.*

Fine, he told me. A clock was apt to illustrate the movements of the skies. *After all*, he said, *parts should commune with parts as they seem to do. But remise the metaphor and you're suddenly wrong. It runs one way and one only. We pertain to stars, but can you tell me how we're meant to touch them?*

I said nothing.

His jowls buckled. *Your answer'd come quick,* and here neither grimace nor grin, *if I asked you to explain your contraptions.* He lifted his book between us. In the ambient light that was left he translated one line aloud. *Parts of the universe too, we may yet make recourse to angels.*

So they go, but what should I call them? The *orbiter dicta* of his *éminence grise*. There.

I walked away with him still chuffing from the pepperbox toward the rudder's wakes.

Returned to my cabin. Tried to recall what prayers I half remembered.

Palpitant ruckus. He favors his heels and his sabot step daubed the deckboards, trebled by the interchangeable rings on his belt. He hasn't fastened the same book to it twice.

Sententiae antiquae. Psalms, epigrams, *shlokas*. Tomorrow dialogues in Greek, then fables and *kōan*.

I muttered as many errant Hail Marys as I could for his casuist soul.

Ported. We've come ashore windward in the Grenadines. Safe from sermonettes, I write from a watchtower. Or what was. A converted observatory on a volcano's edge.

I poured myself up the mountainside on liquefied legs. Cragged, anfractuous, a slope that bites and looks bitten plateaus toward a study in mint, composed with steam. Brumous. Calor and damp transact, wrinkle the treetops. Sagittal plants strain skyward. With an admittance like mercy, some melt into blue.

The tower a panoptic axis. Here I heard a legend.

For the Kalinago who built it, the volcano was the febrile headspring of all that their sky had been. Its first eruption emitted the sun. Then a cycle of winds swept the sun away. Tussive plumes of coal came billowing after. Among them shrapnel. Pumice and spitfire pitch so hot they still strobe. And these became their constellations. They stood for lifetimes looking up from the tower to learn them.

If an axis, an apex too. A vantage on a triangle trade. The island at the convergence of arms that hold it by the throat.

Slaves sow and reap sugarcane for rum shipped to Europe, traded for muslin, for cloaks of Guinea cloth exchanged in Africa for slaves who'll come and cut cane for rum.

To speak of coercion would be an undue kindness. Slavers drive them onto ships with crops of hippopotamus hide. Stuff them shoulder to shoulder in the holds. Crimped and crimped again at hard angles like generously drawn ems flipped on their sides. Bisected, tied in place across the chest. Up to their ankles in rank wastewater and bilge.

And whither revenue there follows war. Ours with the French and both sides by proxy. From the tower each watched for the other's attacks. Now a watchful peace between us. And the privateers we paid defect from their letters of marque. They prowl the archipelagos. Loot shipments of liquor, bottle and cask. Cache what they can't carry on sandbanks surrounded by reefs arrayed like *chevaux-de-frise*.

Come nightfall all above was an inverted vale and the drops of dew upon it fire. I can only think the legend had it right.

Awoke to mock rapture. A troupe of heathen tambourines. The priest picking his way up the emery cliffs rattled like a pack mule, one laden with pots and pans. Instruments, some in cases, some out, slung every which way over his chest. His back a cairn of saddlebags.

Would you could see what he scummed together.

A balsa wood panel. He'd written a zero on its middle and jigsawed it free. Hip-high, a telescope angled up and sharply so. Under its eyepiece, he clamped the panel. That darkened a quarto of parchment farther down, drawn taut across the little lap desk he wore all the way here on a threadbare strap. He crouched beside it like a supplicant.

The telescope beamed the sun, a single florin, on the parchment. *Moiré* with miniscule sinews lit up inside the overcast. The priest watched and waited. Waited and watched cross-eyed for a flaw to break off from the umbra and float into the light. A cantrip, a trick of mirrors. Transit of Venus.

Where we observe one planet, for centuries Greek astronomers saw two. Hesperus and Phosphorus, depending on when they were looking. At dusk or at dawn. Children of Eos. She, of the famous rosy fingers.

Phosphorus. In Latin, Lucifer, *verbatim*. Isiah's exiled seraph, insurrectionist, tempter. How far we've come from love.

Transits occur but rarely. Two-hundred-and-forty-three years apart. I'm told it's Avicenna who witnessed one first. In 1032.

And it will look like that, he told me. *A flaw*, he said. Six hours adrift from side to side.

All his figuring depends on distance, all his distance contingent on parallax.

As many transits as observers observing across the earth. From San Tome and Tripolitsa. Île Bourbon, Van Dieman's Land. Choose two and halve the space between them. Extend an imaginary line from wherever that is to Venus.

Savage abstraction. It goes on like that. Rearranged equations. Ratios applied. One triangle closes where another one opens. Soon enough, the interstice between us and the sun's become a datum.

I wonder, how long does an axiom last? Fortune's face is always changing.

Before we attained the harbor and made anchorage, the sea clock predicted our arrival by a negligible fraction of a mile. Right on time, the island breached the surface far out in front of us, algaed, drab green, like the back of a whale, and froze.

The priest curled up, a question mark, over his tabulations. His a more hesitant estimate, hours in the making. By then, distended spinnakers and running downwind, the measure he took of our position had changed.

I keep thinking he competes with himself for a losing place.

Volte face.

Kalends again and tonight by torchlight we reembark. If I could, I'd turn the clock ahead and have the ship go with it.

The trees are suddenly alive with owls. Otherworldly moans intrude on grunting and shoves. An odd huff interspersed. Three of the crew lean blistered shoulders into the capstan's spokes. Ferrous creaks call back and the anchors rise.

Trysails up a quarter-day out. Bad weather behind us hies us home. A short sea that follows. Waves kerf the bottoms out from under one another. The keel can't decide to hog or to sag.

Hippotes held the winds imprisoned in a bull's-hide sack. All was well until someone let go the closures.

We're routed. An advanced band of mosquitos has broken off from a swarm that had the harbor under siege. Stolen aboard, they've penetrated the hold and now insinuate themselves among us, consorting uninvited with all of our flesh.

A flatus keyed high over the pestilent hiss of fruit flies newly hatched from the barrels of sweetsops and Spanish limes that we loaded. Somewhere a coconut's gone rogue and ricochets from one bulkhead to the next.

I've just checked in and wound the clock. Back in my cabin, the crystals blooming in the storm glass flutter. Next comes a twinge in my thumb. A cavalcade gait and a knock at my door.

I hadn't looked up when I heard.

Join me again on the deck?

EPILOGUE

b[   ] disgorged [ ]n a lone atoll sickly green where
the tides retrieve it [   ] omens smolder in the
carcass of [   ] wrecked skiff [   ] that I
burned [   ] the wind plays through its ribs
like an oud [
                                    ] I couldn't say for what
I could have hoped [   ] and couldn't say I didn't or [
                                                      ] tell them
was [   ] and isn't [   ]
that [   ] sixty seconds' worth of ticks [   ] and twenty-six
sounds are not enough to say [   ] but here's
sweet juice from softer reeds I'll [   ]t with halloos at the
water's edge un[   ] answer[   ]
howl of saltgrass anthems [   ]d bide my time
carving calendar notches in a bone baton [   ] these bottles
[   ] roll billets doux in every one [
         ] I'll wear a haw crown [   ] bray helter-
skelter and live on lotus hips [   ]ays
believing all the voices that I've been [   ]n walk out
[   ] the waves [   ] fistful of coral viatica
and drink me till I dro[   ]

www.ingramcontent.com/pod-product-compliance
Lightning Source LLC
Chambersburg PA
CBHW031420160426
43196CB00008B/1004